The Parachut[e]

The Sto[ry of]

Reverend George Edward Maule Parry A.K.C

4 February 1915 to 6 June 1944
Curate of the parish of St John the Baptist, Leytonstone
12 June 1938 to 6 July 1940

John Wilson

The Parachuting Parson
Copyright ©2016 John Wilson
ISBN 978-1-326-64504-5

The right of John Wilson to be identified as the author of this work has been asserted by him in accordance with the Copyright, Designs and Patents Act 1988.

No part of this book may be used or reproduced or transmitted in any form or by any means, electronic or mechanical including photocopying, recording or by any information storage and retrieval system, without the express written permission of the author, except for brief quotations, which must be properly accredited.

Preface

Greater love has no one than this, that he lay down his life for his friends. *John 15 v13*

It is not often that the discovery, in a junk shop, of a battered old wartime suitcase triggers the telling of the story of a local war hero, but that is the providential circumstance with regard to the Reverend Captain George Parry. The suitcase was discovered in 2014 by Jenni Crane and has uncovered a story that is really worth telling: the long overdue account of his life, faith and heroism.

In his all too short life, George Parry proved to be a highly able parish priest, an effective army chaplain and most certainly a war hero. He died on D-Day 1944, seeking to protect the injured British soldiers to whom God had called him to minister. After the example of his Lord and Saviour, *he laid down his life for his friends.*

On July 9, in the same year, Right Reverend James Inskip, one of my predecessors, spoke at his memorial service. As the current Bishop of Barking I am honoured to write this preface to this inspiring record of his life, carefully researched by John Wilson of St John's Parish Church, Leytonstone where Padre Parry, as he became known, served his curacy. Doubly so, in that like me and Jenni Crane, who discovered the suitcase, Padre Parry is of Welsh heritage.

The Bishop of Chelmsford who ordained him in 1938 described George as *"one of the best and most promising young men who ever entered Holy Orders."* After his curacy in St John's Leytonstone, where he was extremely popular, and a brief time as parish priest at Emmanuel Forest Gate, like many young clergy Parry volunteered to be an army chaplain. On June 6, 1944, at the age of 29, as a chaplain to the 6th Airborne Division, and in the dead of night, Captain Parry parachuted in to northern France close to the enemy lines, where over the next few hours the story of his heroism unfolded. That is the story that awaits you in these pages.

I very much wish I could have known him, but in the reading of this little booklet *we shall remember him.*

+ Peter Barking

Right Reverend Peter Hill
Bishop of Barking

Early Years

George Edward Maule Parry was born on February 4, 1915 in Hornchurch, Essex. He was the firstborn of Reverend Allen James Parry and his wife Muriel.

Allen James Parry, born in 1873 in Llangattock Lingoed in Monmouthshire, was the son of a farmer. He worked in this district as a corn merchant's clerk for several years before moving to London and taking Holy Orders. During his third curacy, he married Muriel Constance St. John Maule on January 15, 1914. Just over a year later, George was born. The couple then had three more sons: Allen, born in 1916, Roden in 1917, and Peter in 1919. In 1917, Reverend Allen Parry became a Temporary Chaplain to the Forces and a year later he became vicar of St Peter's Upton Cross, where he stayed until he retired.

George's mother Muriel was the daughter of George and Emily Maule. Her father was an officer in the Royal Artillery, and rose to the rank of Lieutenant Colonel before he retired. Muriel's sister, Florence, was born in Bombay (Mumbai, India) in 1880. The family moved back to England and Muriel was born in February 1882 in Torquay, Devon.

Not much is known about George's formative years, but we do know a little about his education. His parents sent George to Farnfield's Preparatory School, which was a boarding school in Bickley, Kent. No record of a school by this name has been found; however, the Farnfields were a well-known family of schoolmasters. Samuel Farnfield had taught at and run a number of schools before starting a Preparatory School in Sidcup Hall in 1907. A move to Bickley Hall was planned but Samuel Farnfield passed away in 1918 before the move could be implemented. The school was run with the help of two of his sons, Archibald John Farnfield and Bernard Samuel Farnfield. These two sons ran the school when it moved to Bickley Hall later that year. The school continued there until after the Second World War. Kelly's directory of Kent for 1927 says this school was off Chislehurst Road and was being run by Samuel Farnfield's sons, Archibald and Bernard. This school is the most likely candidate to be the Farnfield's Preparatory School, and thus, to be the school that George attended.

The alternative option was set up in 1919 by Reverend J W Blencowe, who had been a field chaplain in Gallipoli in the First World War. It was in the same Sidcup Hall vacated by the previous school. The Headmaster of this school was also a Mr. Farnfield. It is very likely that he was another of Samuel Farnfield's sons. Sidcup Hall and Bickley Hall were not very far from one another.

Tony Orchard attended Bickley Hall School around ten years after George. In his Book, *Here's to Our Far-Flung Empire* he has this to say about the school:

> *Bickley Hall was an archetypal prep school in the London area and competed in both sport and academic records with other similar schools .... I cannot think of a better description of its ethos and what it was like to be there than the Hogwarts School of Harry Potter fame .... Bickley Hall had it all: houses (Grey and Cerise after the school colours), a Latin motto, in Domino confide (in the Lord I trust), dormitories named after British heroes like Scott, Byers, Shackleton and so on, a school chapel of its own, emphasis on the team spirit and conformity ('play up, play up and play the game'), and last but not least the sine qua non for such establishments, bloody awful food.*

George left Prep School in 1928 at the age of 13. In January 1929, he and his brother Allen went on to attend Weymouth College, which was a boarding school in Weymouth, near the dockyard and stood in 20 acres of land. Paton's List of Schools and Tutors (1929) has this to say about the college and what it offered its pupils:

> *Weymouth College is a Public School, established to 'provide for the sons of gentlemen a classical, mathematical, and general education of the highest class'.*
>
> *The religious teaching is on sound Church of England principles.*
>
> *.... There are Classical and Modern sides, but Science and Latin are taught in all lower forms. Spanish and Drawing are also in the curriculum. Extras include music, the organ, handicrafts, shorthand and book-keeping.*

Picture 1: Weymouth College. Courtesy of Dorset History Centre

The choice of Weymouth College may have been assisted by the fact that the Bishop of Barking, Right Reverend James Inskip, who knew the family, was the chairman of the school council at the college. It was also owned by Evangelical Church Schools Ltd.

George appears to have been a keen thespian as he took part in three Shakespeare productions for the Lower School at the college, *Henry VI* pt. II in 1929, *Midsummer Night's Dream* in 1930 and *The Tempest* in 1931. He also took part in a number of other plays for his form. George was a member of the Weymouth College Field Club, its debating society and the college's Officer Training Corps. However, he does not seem to have been inclined towards sports. The only record shows him coming in 47th out of 52 in the steeplechase one year.

Picture 2: Some of the cast from Midsummer Night's Dream. George is on the left. Courtesy of Dorset History Centre.

George left Weymouth College in July 1933. All four brothers attended Weymouth College, so it is possible that they may have attended the same prep school. The College was closed in 1940, because it was dangerously close to the dockyard that had become a target for bombing by the Luftwaffe.

As his father had done before him, George went on to complete his education at King's College London, which he entered to study for the Associateship in 1933. He graduated in 1937.

In Holy Orders

The decision for George to go into the priesthood may have been made at an early age. As mentioned earlier, the teaching at Weymouth College was on sound Church of England principles and there was a connection to the Diocese of Chelmsford through the Bishop of Barking. The associateship at King's College London was also a common path to the priesthood, which his father had also taken. The final part of George's journey to becoming a priest was at Bishop's College, Cheshunt, where he trained for Holy Orders. The trustees of the college were the Bishops of St. Albans, London, Southwark and Chelmsford.

After leaving Bishop's College, George was ordained Deacon on June 12, 1938 and was the Gospeller for the ordination service in Chelmsford Cathedral. He was appointed Curate of St. John the Baptist Church, Leytonstone under Canon William Brown, the Vicar of St. John's.

In the parish magazine for June 1938, Canon Brown wrote:

> *On Trinity Sunday, June 12th, Mr. George Parry is to be Ordained and Licenced to the Curacy of St. John's. I know you will give him a hearty welcome and make him feel at home with us. I hope Mr. Parry will devote himself to the work amongst young people. I feel in many ways this is really the most important of all church work and alas! It is the one which is giving the authorities of the Church the greatest anxiety.*

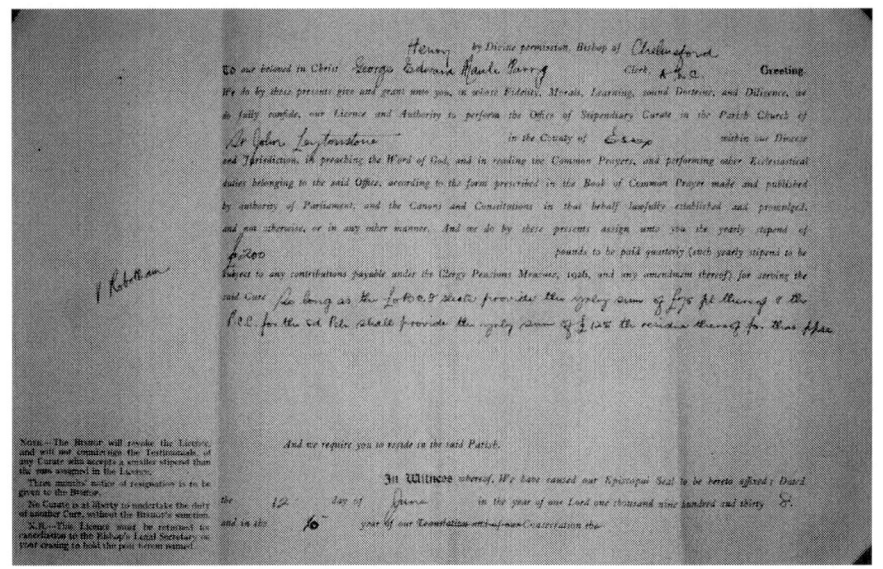

Picture 3: The Curates Licence issued upon George's appointment as Curate to St. John's Leytonstone. Courtesy of Chelmsford Diocese and Essex Record Office.

George Parry's involvement with the youth of St. John's was already being planned before his arrival. In the same magazine, his name is mentioned in connection with the planned Sunday School Treat to Southend on July 2. He was to write about his experience of this in the August issue of the magazine. The trip was by train and on the way back the children in his carriage started a paper chase and he became a target for "such paper as was left over".

In September, a letter was to appear in *The Times* under the heading "Moral Rearmament". The authors of the letter were prominent people of the time. In it they state:

> The real need of the day is therefore moral and spiritual rearmament. A growing body of people in this and other countries are making it their aim. It is a work in which all men and women, in all countries and of all races are called to share and have power to help. Were we, together with our fellow men everywhere, to put the energy and resourcefulness into this task that we now find

> *ourselves obliged to expend on national defence, the peace of the world would be assured.*

The letter was in response to the issues in the world at that time and, in particular, how events in Europe were unfolding and the general feeling that it was heading towards a new war. George had the complete letter reprinted in the October Parish Magazine. In his introduction to it he says:

> *Let it be remembered that we become active workers for the peace of the world when that deep-seated acceptance of the life of our Lord becomes the governing factor of our lives.*

George was neither promoting appeasement nor advocating war. He was saying that if we truly accept Christ as Lord we become active participants (and the stress is on active) in working for the peace of the world. Accepting Christ does not make us bystanders; we are stronger when Christians of all nations, races and denominations put the effort into working together for the good of humanity and the world.

At the beginning of 1939, George set up St. John's Confirmation School to prepare children for confirmation. The school was intended to run for three terms of 10 weeks each, coinciding with the secular school terms and held at the church. He also restarted the Communicants Guild at St. John's to help communicants, new and old alike, prepare for communion.

One of the candidates for confirmation was a fourteen-year-old girl called Daphne Horne, who lived with her sister and parents in a part of Grove Green Road, just outside the parish. In her book, "One Single Poppy", Daphne Carr (nee Horne) recalls that the family attended a service at St. John's around the time of her birthday in November 1938. She was immediately attracted to the young priest preaching from the pulpit. If this was the Sunday after her birthday, George was preaching on the subject of patience. Daphne was not a regular attendee at St. John's at this time. It was her friend Marion

Swenson, a young Sunday school teacher, who encouraged Daphne to join the Sunday school and come regularly to St. John's in February 1939. Marion Swenson would eventually be in charge of St. John's Kindergarten.

On Trinity Sunday 1939, June 4, George Parry was ordained as a priest at Chelmsford Cathedral.

Throughout that year, George continued to be active with the youth of the church. He was involved with Youth Socials and the 21st anniversary celebrations of the Young Peoples Society, Majors and Minors, of which he was chairman. He was also involved in other youth groups including the Children's Guild and the Sunday school. In addition, he ran the Sunday school teachers' preparation class.

George chaired the team organising the Sunday school treat to be held on July 1 that year. Imagine the scene, early on a summer morning, as more than ninety children and adults snaked their way down from the church towards Leytonstone High Road Station to catch the train to Thorpe Bay. Writing in the August issue of the Parish Magazine he says:

> *That we all arrived on the beach at Thorpe Bay was due, not to any outward display of discipline, but to a common thought in the minds of all that that was the final aim of this expedition.*

Daphne Carr recalls that George decided to go swimming in the sea and when he came out he was shivering. She offered him her coat, but he refused to take it. The water may have been cold, but it was a sunny day and by all accounts this day at the beach, with races and prizes was enjoyed by all and everyone was tired as they journeyed home. He ends his article in the August 1939 magazine by saying:

> *In conclusion, Julius Caesar once said 'Veni, Vidi, Vici', the writer of this article is constantly saying 'Veni, Vidi, Victus Sum'. (I came, I saw, I was overcome.)*

George did not only work with the youth of St John's. He was active with the whole of church. He often attended and participated in meetings of the Mothers' Union and also went with them on their outings. He promoted the Diocesan News Team Rally in the parish and he also became the point of contact for St John's involvement in the plans for the Chelmsford Diocese 25th anniversary pageant play. The play was due to run for two weeks from September 23, at the Scala Theatre, Charlotte Street in London, but was cancelled at short notice when war broke out.

On September 3, 1939, the day war broke out, Canon W. T. Brown, the Vicar of St. John's, passed away and George was put in temporary charge of the parish. Canon Brown's death was not a surprise. He had been unwell for some time and had not taken a service at St. John's since the end of July. The appointment of Reverend John Stanley was announced in the November Parish magazine, but he did not take up the position until January 1940. The early announcement of Canon Brown's replacement may indicate that the need for one was already being considered before his death.

The Bishop of Barking, the Right Reverend James Inskip, describes this time in the obituary he wrote for George Parry, published in *The Times* on July 1, 1944:

> *His vicar died on the day that war began and George was severely tested in having to take charge of an important parish while still scarcely fledged. He won the love of the people, as he did some months later when he took charge of a Forest Gate parish, whose vicar was a chaplain to the forces.*

Throughout his stay at St. John's George had lodged with Mr. and Mrs. Foster of 10 Cambridge Road. In February 1940, he moved to

Langford, Bushwood. His parents would also move to Bushwood when his father retired. They were to move to Norfolk Place, 14 Bushwood, not far from St. John's Vicarage.

In his first vicar's letter, published in the February 1940 magazine, Reverend John Stanley announced that George Parry would be leaving St. John's to take up a curacy in Prittlewell. However, by March, that had changed as the Bishop of Chelmsford had appointed him to take over as Priest in Charge of Emmanuel, Forest Gate. The vicar of Emmanuel, Forest Gate, Reverend Joost de Blank, was waiting to be called up as an Army Chaplain. News that the vicar of Emmanuel church had finally received his papers broke in April 1940. Even so, Reverend de Blank did not leave Emmanuel church until June and it was July when George finally took up his new post.

The young Daphne Horne was now fifteen. Her feelings for George had grown and she had looked forward to the confirmation classes, which were often held in his lodgings. They had come to an end in December 1939, when she had been confirmed at All Hallows by the Tower, the church in which she and her sister had been baptised. She missed the confirmation classes and the opportunity they gave her to be in his presence.

The news that George would be leaving St. John's upset her even more. She decided to orchestrate a meeting with him. Daphne

Picture 4: Daphne Horne aged 15. Courtesy of Bernard Carr

told George she had a number of questions about the bible and Christianity that she wanted to ask and he agreed to meet with her and discuss them. They sat on either side of a table in his lodgings and discussed a list of questions that she had put together with the help of her father. Daphne Carr recalls that he showed no sign of any feelings towards her and he ended the meeting when she came to the end of her list of questions. She left disappointed that she could not bring herself to say how she felt.

In June 1940, George's brother Allen, who had been in France with the Essex regiment, came back home having been evacuated from Dunkirk.

Picture 5: The four Parry brothers, outside St Peter's Vicarage. From left to right, Peter, Roden, Allen and George. Courtesy of Bernard Carr.

George's last Sunday at St. John's was to be June 30. He preached at both the morning and evening services. The following Saturday St. John's said their good-byes to him at their Garden Fete, where he was presented with a cigarette case, a gift that he wanted so he could carry it with him for the rest of his life. It was wartime and many children had been evacuated. There was to be no Sunday school treat to the seaside that year.

In the month of his leaving, Vi Gilbert from the Young People's Society at St. John's wrote this about him in the parish magazine:

> No words can truly express what we owe to Mr. Parry's inspiring influence in his work with us, especially this winter. In no circumstances, however dark, has he ever done otherwise than radiate cheerfulness and hope amongst us.

For a young man of 25 years of age and only two years as a curate to be given charge of a parish would have been unusual, but it was wartime and a number of priests had joined up to be Forces Chaplains. George's four months in charge of St. John's, after the death of Canon Brown, may have helped the Bishop of Chelmsford in his choice. His father was also vicar of the neighbouring parish of St Peter's, Upton Cross, but that is unlikely to have influenced the decision. George was rated highly by the Right Reverend Henry Wilson, Bishop of Chelmsford, who, after George's death had this to say about his potential in the Chelmsford Chronicle of June 30, 1944:

> .... I ordained George at Chelmsford Cathedral in 1938 and he was one of the best and most promising young men who ever entered Holy Orders.

In September 1940, George visited Daphne Horne's parents at their home in Grove Green Road. Daphne was unaware of the visit as she was in the garden and did not see him until he was about to leave. A few days later a land mine damaged their house and the Horne's were forced to move. After a short stay at their cousin's house in Billericay Daphne and her family moved to Shenfield.

Around the time of her sixteenth birthday, in November 1940, Daphne decided to visit George at his new church, Emmanuel Forest Gate. She and her mother took the bus and arrived at a nearly empty church shortly before the end of the morning service. When the service was over, George walked back to the bus stop with them. After he left, Daphne told her mother that she will live to see the day when George will love her and belong to her.

George's stay at Emmanuel Forest Gate was short-lived. Like his predecessor, he too was to join the Royal Army Chaplains Department (RAChD) and become a Chaplain to the Forces. However, his time at the church was not uneventful. It was the time of the Blitz and he had to deal with matters after the church was hit by an incendiary bomb on December 3, 1940. He also arranged for the fitting of blackout curtains so that early morning services could still be held in the church.

On Boxing Day, 1940 George made a visit to the Horne family at their home in Shenfield. He visited again a few days later, on January 11, this time with his mother. Daphne Carr recalls her disappointment that he still appeared to be indifferent towards her. He asked if he could visit the family again on February 22, two days before he was due to join the Army Chaplains training course. As he left her home he asked Daphne if she would write to him whilst he was away in the army.

Chaplain to the Forces

George first made his request to be appointed as a Chaplain to the Forces at an interview with the Assistant Chaplain General, Eastern Command, on May 27, 1940, whilst he was still at St. John's. He made a request again three months later and was told that he would be considered when he reached the age of twenty-eight.

In January 1941, shortly before his twenty-sixth birthday, George received a letter from the RAChD enclosing a fresh application form. He was clearly surprised to receive it. In his covering letter of January 22, he says:

> *In view of a previous letter dated Sept 2nd 1940 informing me that no appointment can be made in my case till I reach the age of 28; am I therefore to enclose again another medical certificate and Bishop's recommendation?*
>
> *I do not make this request because I no longer wish to be recommended, but because I do wish most earnestly to do this piece of work. I wish to be clear in my own mind that the enclosed form of application is for me and that there is no mistake, in view of the previous letter referred to.*

There was no mistake. George left Emmanuel, Forest Gate in February 1941. He attended Chaplains Training at the RAChD Training Centre and Depot at Chester and was commissioned Chaplain to the Forces 4th Class (ranking as Captain) on February 24, 1941. Two weeks later, after completing the training course George was attached to 3rd Training Battalion, Royal Army Service Corps (RASC), stationed in Bulford Wiltshire.

Picture 6: Course photo taken at the RAChD Training Centre and Depot, Chester. George is fourth from the right in the back row. Courtesy of the Museum of Army Chaplaincy.

George was the last of the four brothers to serve in the forces. His brother Allen had joined the army in August 1939, followed by Roden in December the same year. Peter joined his brother Allen in the Essex regiment in 1940.

Daphne wrote to George shortly after he left her in February, but he did not reply. Instead, he turned up at her home on April 14, Easter Monday. Whilst walking back to the station he gave her the first indication that he might have feelings for her. Two weeks later, Daphne received a letter from George in which he expressed his love for her. In her book, Daphne Carr writes that she believes that it was her mother who convinced George to say how he felt about her. He was not certain he should, because he did not want Daphne to feel tied to him as he went off to war.

In the first week of June 1941, George went back home on a week's leave. Daphne and her family had been invited to a tea party at the end of May with George's parents and his brothers Allen and Roden; a party that she felt did not go too well. However, she was invited to stay with George's parents whilst he was home on leave. In her book, Daphne Carr recalls the first conversation she had with George upon his arrival at St Peter's vicarage on June 3:

> *Daphne, Mother tells me you are only sixteen, I didn't know that.*
>
> *Well, you don't have to have me.*
>
> *I mean to have you whether you are sixteen or sixty. We will become engaged when you are eighteen and marry when you are twenty.*
>
> *But that's another four years.*

George and Daphne spent time together that week and on Friday, June 6, 1941, George and Daphne went up town with his family. They ate at a place called "Frascati's" and saw the film "Bitter Sweet" at the Empire, Leicester Square.

On the Sunday Daphne, George and his family went to church at St. John's Leytonstone. It was Trinity Sunday and George had been invited to preach at the morning service. They dropped George off at the church then went on to visit Reverend John Stanley at his vicarage before the service. Daphne's mother and sister were also at the church for the service.

The appearance of both families seems to have sparked rumours of an engagement because shortly thereafter George wrote to Daphne's mother expressing his concern about the rumours. George was concerned because he would need the permission of the Bishop of Chelmsford before getting engaged and such rumours could cause problems for both Daphne and him. Between them,

George and Daphne's mother did their best to squash the rumours. The couple did not get engaged.

George returned to Bulford after his leave. Three months later he was sent to West Africa (Gold Coast). He left England on September 15, 1941, arriving on October 24. Once in Africa, George was assigned to 2 Initial Training Centre.

In 1941, the Gold Coast was an important victualing point for ships travelling round the Cape to India and to the Middle East. Until November 1942, neighbouring countries were held by the Vichy French and whilst there were no significant campaigns in the area after 1940 the defence of the Gold Coast was important to Britain's war effort.

George and Daphne corresponded regularly with each other, although the difficultly in sending mail meant that letters would arrive grouped together or there would be no letters for weeks. Soon after he arrived in West Africa, George's youngest brother, Peter, was killed in action at El Duda on November 26, 1941, during the operation to relieve Tobruk.

On May 25, 1942 George was assigned to HQ 5 West African Brigade. Ten months later he was attached to 26 Casualty Clearing Station. This was his last assignment in Africa. In May 1943, he left West Africa. He returned home on June 15, 1943 for 28 days leave.

Whilst George was away, Daphne was growing up. She was now eighteen and was enjoying life to the full. She had started to use make-up and style and colour her hair. She was also going to dances, helping to entertain the American G.I.s and generally having a good time. Daphne regularly visited George's parents. His family, and, in particular, his mother did not approve of the changes in Daphne's lifestyle. The war and growing up had changed both Daphne and George. When they met, after his return from Africa, things did not go well. He did not like the changes he saw in her and how she had behaved whilst he had been away. His experiences in West Africa had probably also changed him. He broke up with her and they were never to see one another again.

From Daphne Carr's book, it appears that both mothers may have had a hand in the romance. Daphne's mother had a hand in getting the pair together, encouraging George to come out with his feelings for Daphne when he was not sure that the timing was right. George's mother may have had a hand in their separation. Daphne Carr says in her book that George's mother had been openly rude to her shortly before he came home from Africa and did not like her. However, the circumstances they found themselves in, in the middle of a global conflict, cannot be ignored.

Whilst on leave George went with his brother Roden to Weymouth. There they visited the Weymouth College Aisle in St. Aldhelm's Church on July 5 and signed the visitors book. Six days later, he visited St. John's and preached at the morning service.

On June 22, a week after he had returned from Africa, George wrote to the Royal Army Chaplains Department to express his preference for his next posting. In his letter he says:

> *I have the honour to report that I am on recuperative leave from West Africa. I wish to submit my name for a posting to the Airborne Division as a parachutist.*
>
> *My reason for making this application now rather than after a posting to some other unit is to avoid the inconvenience caused to all by asking for a transfer.*

George was clearly determined to serve with the Parachute Regiment. He was to be initially disappointed as, after his leave was over, he was attached to the Central Ordnance Depot, Bicester. However, his request had not been ignored. On September 10, he was assigned to the 7th Battalion, Light Infantry, the Parachute Regiment. He was stationed in Bulford, where he had been two years earlier when he was attached to the RASC.

Picture 7: Centre portion of the 7th Para battalion photo. George is fourth from the right in the third row. Courtesy of the Airborne Assault Museum.

On January 26, 1944 the whole of 7th Para were given ten days leave and George went home. His father had retired in late 1943 and his parents were now living in Bushwood, Leytonstone, close to St. John's vicarage. Like all retired priests his father helped out at local churches when needed and he had been helping out at St. John's. He was due to officiate at the 8am Holy Communion on January 30. On his return home George was asked by Reverend John Stanley to preach at the 11am service on the same day. He happily agreed, but, this time, insisted that he would have to ask for a fee. The fee would be going to the Airborne Forces Benevolent Fund.

On May 19, 7th Para went to Brigmeiston Fields where they were part of a parade of airborne troops inspected by King George VI and other members of the Royal Family. A week later, the battalion moved from Bulford to Tilshead in Wiltshire in readiness of D-Day.

D-Day

In 1944, the Allies were preparing for Operation Overlord and retaking Europe from the Axis forces. On June 5, the battalion moved to Fairford Park, near to Fairford airfield, in preparation for their part in the action. The unit War Diary for that day records that George held a short outdoor service. The actor Richard Todd, then a Lieutenant in 7th Para, has this to say about that Service:

> *As the shadows lengthened on Monday, June 5, the stand-to order was given. The last ceremony that day was a drumhead service in a meadow near Fairford Airfield by our popular padre, Captain Parry, known to us all as Pissy Percy the Parachuting Parson. Parry was a wiry little Welshman with a nature as fiery as his red hair, and a heart and courage to match. Drawn-up in a semi-circle, 610 men faced inwards towards the padre who stood on an ammunition box. A more unlikely or piratical congregation could not be imagined, every man abristle with weapons, his face and hands besmirched with black cream, his helmet on the ground before him, his rifle or Sten gun laid across it. Onward Christian Soldiers went well. Abide With Me was rather more ragged. It was not easy to sing that in such a setting and at such a moment.*

At 1900 hours the battalion moved to the airfield and at 2320 hours it took off for Normandy.

The 6th Airborne Division, of which 7th Para was a part, were tasked with capturing and holding vital targets behind enemy lines. 7th Para's targets were the bridges codenamed "Pegasus" and "Horsa". There were two waterways, the River Orne and the Caen Canal that ran parallel to each other. The only crossing point was two bridges, one over each waterway. The Coup de Main force, under Major Howard, who were to capture the bridges, landed in six gliders around thirty minutes ahead of the main force. The drop zone for 7th Para was near Ranville on the east side of the River Orne. Benouville was on the west side of the canal bridge. This bridgehead was to be held by them at all costs, until relieved.

Picture 8: Reconnaissance photo of Pegasus Bridge. The triangular area above the bridge is the landing zone for the Coup de Main force. Part of Benouville is visible in the bottom right corner. Courtesy of the Airborne Assault Museum.

Picture 9: Reconnaissance photo of the Horsa Bridge. Courtesy of the Airborne Assault Museum.

The Battalion was dropped from Stirling's over Ranville around 0100 hours June 6, 1944. Stirling's were bombers and the exit through which the men were to jump has been described as a large coffin-shaped aperture in the floor of the tail of the plane. With their kit and parachutes, it was not easy for the men as they prepared to jump through a hole in the floor with the planes buffeting around and evading flak.

Picture 10: Reconnaissance photo of the drop zone for 7th Para. Ranville is visible in the bottom right corner. Courtesy of the Airborne Assault Museum.

The pilots had problems locating the drop zone and with strong winds affecting the descent the battalion was scattered. Once on the ground, the cloud cover and consequent lack of moonlight made it more difficult for the men to locate the rendezvous point (RV). Initially caught by surprise, the enemy soon recovered and fought back. In his news article for the Daily Sketch on June 29, 1944 Leonard Moseley had this to say:

> *The Parachute Division was given the job in the early hours of D-Day of dropping by parachute and capturing intact the vital bridges spanning the River Orne and the Caen Canal. Padre Parry dropped with them. Soon all were engaged in defending themselves against some of the bitterest and most determined Nazi counter-attacks of the invasion.*

In the chaos of war, it was some time before even half of the battalion had reached the RV. The unit War Diary entry for 0100 hours records that it went into action with companies at half normal strength due to some plane loads being dropped in wrong places, or not being dropped at all. In his diary (adapted by Barbara Maddox in her book, *The Tale of two Bridges*, Lieutenant Colonel Pine-Coffin the Commanding Officer of 7th Para says:

> *Myself and Lieutenant Rogers collected many wanderers in their search for the RV. It was a most desperate feeling to know that one was so close to it, but not knowing in which direction it lay.*

It was almost by chance that they located the RV and that was in part due to a flare being dropped, probably from one of the bombers, which lit up the area briefly, allowing them to see the distinctive church in Ranville across the fields. The bugler was with the Colonel and was playing the signal in the hope that it would gather the battalion together. Lieutenant Rogers also had the green lantern. Of course, both could also attract the enemy as well as friends.

7th Para was under attack from the moment they started to land. It is possible that George was moving amongst them and offering encouragement and may have been helping to gather them together. At some point, with the battalion only about half strength, Lieutenant Colonel Pine-Coffin decided they could not wait any longer and issued orders for the three companies to move out.

There is significant uncertainty over exactly when 7th Para reached the bridges. Some sources say it was as early as 0130 hours, others after 0300 hours. The planned time of arrival was 0130 hours and everything did not go according to the plan. It seems unlikely that, barring a few individuals, this was when the battalion arrived in any strength. In his diary, Pine-Coffin mentions taking his force over the canal bridge at 0140 hours and later that the leading troops crossed the canal at 0240 hours. Other sources are equally unhelpful. While the battalion were taking their positions, George was probably on his way to Ranville with some of the battalion's medics. The battalion doctor, Captain Young, was missing.

Sometime around 0300 hours, George reached the Chateau in Ranville, where the Main Dressing Station was being set up by 225 Field Ambulance. Ranville was near the drop zone on the east side of the waterways. It had been taken by 13th Battalion at around 0230 hours. Major Hewlings was in charge at the Dressing Station and George may have informed him that Captain Young had not shown up at the RV. In his book, *The Pegasus and Orne Bridges: Their Capture, Defence and Relief on D-Day*, Neil Barber says:

> Captain Young, the 7th Battalion Doctor, had failed to turn up at the RV, and so Major Hewlings ordered Captain John Wagstaff to take a group consisting of nine personnel of 2 Section and five reinforcements from 4 Section to form the 7th Battalion RAP in Benouville. Also in with this group were a few 7th Battalion medical personnel brought up by their Padre, George Parry.

The battalion took up their positions with 'A' Company in Benouville and 'B' Company in Le Port. 'C' Company was used more flexibly in support of the other companies and in reserve. The entry in the unit war diary for 0325 hours records:

> Bn occupied objective and held it against various counter-attacks "A" and "B" Coys being heavily engaged. Cas - killed 3 Officers, Capt Parry (Padre), Lt Bowyer and Lt Hill, and 16

ORs. Wounded 4 Officers, Major TAYLOR, Capt WEBBER, Lt HUNTER & Lt TEMPLE & 38 ORs. Missing, 170 ORs did not R.V. after drop.

Picture 11: Post War picture of the Horsa Bridge. Courtesy of the Imperial War Museum.

The entry implies that the battalion was in position by 0325 hours. That may have been the case, but it also reflects the results of events that occurred throughout the day. The numbers of missing persons and casualties would not have been known at that time. The battalion fought all day and there is no further mention of casualties for June 6. George certainly had not been killed at this time.

7th Para was undermanned and without heavy weapons support, as the containers holding these weapons had not been located at the drop zone. 'A' Company was under severe pressure from enemy attacks. Leonard Moseley describes the situation:

> *Hearing that 'A' Company of the battalion holding the perimeter of our defences along the west side of the canal near the village of Le Port, was in sore straits and aid for the wounded was badly needed, Padre Parry set off through the darkness to join them.*

Picture 12: A Post War picture of the Pegasus Bridge from the Benouville side. The Coup de Main force gliders are visible to the right of the bridge. Courtesy of the Imperial War Museum.

Moseley provides no timings in his article, but his reference to George probably places this at around the time he was heading to Benouville with the medical team under Captain Wagstaff. Moseley also confuses the two villages on the west bank of the canal bridge.

Crossing the bridge from Ranville, Le Port was to the right and Benouville, where 'A' Company were, was to the left.

Neil Barber says that the medical personnel, including George Parry, under the command of Captain Wagstaff of 225 Field Ambulance, crossed the Orne bridge around 0400 hours and the canal bridge about half an hour later. Wagstaff directed George and some of the medics who had come with them from Ranville to set up an aid post for walking wounded at number 32 on the lower road in Benouville. Wagstaff set up another aid post at number 34. Not long after 'A' Company became cut off from the rest of the battalion and were to remain so for much of the rest of the day.

Leonard Moseley's narrative continues:

> Not long after he (George) arrived Nazi forces infiltrated between the company and the rest of the battalion, cutting them off from all help.
>
> Soon after dawn a Panther tank and self-propelled gun opened fire on them, taking a heavy toll of the men.

In Appendix I of the War Diary Pine-Coffin identifies the tank as a Panzer IV, not a Panther tank, which is more likely.

'A' Company's commander was so badly wounded that he carried on direction of the battle from a stretcher.

Both aid posts quickly filled up and where George was they were dealing with more than just walking wounded. Bill Law, interviewed by Neil Barber for his book, was wounded and made his way to the aid post at number 32. He says:

> The first person I saw actually was Reverend Parry. He was mostly at that time looking after the wounded. He said, 'We've got no room here', 'cos they were all laying about. Of course they couldn't even get them under cover, so they built up part of it with

a canvas, like a tent, and they had a lot of them in that. He said, 'Could you become walking wounded?' 'Yes, I can walk but I've got a couple of bullets in my shoulder.' He said, 'They won't be taken out here.' I thought 'What did you say that for?' 'Well in that case you can be taken back to England.' I said, 'Are you joking?' He said, 'No, there's a hospital ship waiting out there to take you back to England.' They had no more room there they had so many wounded.

According to Neil Barber, it was around 0730 hours that Germans approached the aid post set up by Wagstaff. Most of the wounded and the medical personnel had been moved to the upper floor at number 34 and the Germans did not appear to have seen them. They looked around and after speaking with the owners of the house continued along the lower road towards the aid post at number 32, where George was. Wagstaff, quoted in Neil Barbers' book, says:

> *The Germans continued up the road and entered the other RAP house. A fight ensued, during which several medical people and wounded were killed. Having put up a terrific struggle, the Padre, George Parry was also killed. The patrol then moved on towards the Mairie.*

Leonard Moseley describes the attack in his article:

> *All efforts to get help from the rest of the battalion failed and many men died trying to get through.*
>
> *And then after one attack the enemy broke 'A' Company's line at one point and penetrated sufficiently to reach the medical aid post where Padre Parry was working on the wounded.*
>
> *Those who were near enough to see what happened say that the Nazi troops, who seemed to be in a completely frenzied condition, set upon the wounded shooting and bayoneting them.*

> *Padre Parry immediately went to the aid of the helpless Britons lying on the dressing station floor.*
>
> *He protested vehemently against the murder of the helpless paratroopers and when this was ignored by the enraged Germans he is believed to have tried physical intervention and put himself between the Nazis and the wounded troops.*
>
> *He was then charged by the enemy troops and in the struggle that followed bayonets or knives were used by the Nazis and Padre Parry was cut down. He fell beside the men he tried to save.*
>
> *Owing to the desperate situation that prevailed at the time it was impossible for anyone else in 'A' Company to go to his aid or to the aid of their comrades, and for several hours afterwards the medical post was in no man's land.*

We will never know why the German troops killed everyone in the RAP. What we do know is that George died of bayonet or knife wounds whilst trying to defend his wounded companions – there were no survivors. The RAP was not retaken by 7th Para until later that day.

The battalion were without radio sets, as none had been located when they dropped. A number of runners had tried to get through to the H.Q. without success. In the end, the company's second in command, Captain Jim Webber, although wounded, set off to find battalion H.Q. and inform them of the desperate position 'A' Company was in. He eventually made his way through and told them the situation. Leonard Moseley continues:

> *Not till later in the morning did the second in command of the company manage to reach battalion headquarters and tell his story.*

> *Despite his wounded shoulder, he crawled through the gardens and shell-wrecked houses of Le Port and dodged through the Nazi lines until he reached the bridge.*
>
> *There he refused to have his wound dressed, but asked for a patrol, and immediately returned to his company fighting the whole way back. It was this patrol which recaptured the medical post and occupied it. They found all of its occupants dead, with Padre Parry lying beside them.*
>
> *Then with this small reinforcement 'A' Company held off all subsequent Nazi attacks until late in the evening of D-Day, when troops from the beaches fought their way through and relieved them.*

Moseley again misidentifies the village as the Le Port, but his description generally agrees with the other accounts. The timing of Webber's report is also uncertain. Moseley says late morning, Neil Barber suggests it was mid-afternoon and in the War Diary, Lieutenant Colonel Pine-Coffin says these events took place around 1900 hours. The reinforcement mentioned by Moseley was a platoon from 'C' Company consisting of just 17 men.

Fighting in the villages around the bridges continued all day and it was not until 2115 hours that soldiers from the beaches managed to fight their way through to 7th Para. Lieutenant Todd has this to say about the situation they found themselves in:

> *While the mighty invasion from the sea was being fought out, quite a lot, on a smaller but no less deadly scale, was going on in the 7th Para area. There was no cessation in the Germans' probing with patrols and counter-attacks, some led by tanks, and the regimental aid post was overrun in the early hours. The wounded being tended there were all killed where they lay. So too was Padre Parry, who had evidently fought like a tiger to defend them.*

It is not surprising that the times some events occurred are confused. All reports of the day were written later and those involved had more important tasks to do than to note down the details of every event as it happened. We rely on the memories of those who were there and they were under great pressure. The fact that people's recollections of that day differ is due to the differing situations each one of them faced. It does not reduce the value of their memories. Sometimes the exact time something happens is less important than where it fits in on a timeline of events. This account of events surrounding Reverend George Parry's death tries to put them in a logical order.

Many accounts of that day by men of 7th Para say that George was very popular and his death was sorely felt. Leonard Moseley concludes his article by saying:

> *I was with the men of the battalion during many hours of D-Day watching their successful battle to hold the bridge and I know how deeply they felt the loss of the man who had dropped with them in the dangerous darkness of the night before.*
>
> *I don't think there was a man in the whole battalion who that day did not fight to avenge the death of Padre Parry.*

Picture 13: An aerial view of the two bridges taken after D-Day. Pegasus Bridge is bottom right and the Coup de Main gliders are visible next to it. Horsa Bridge is centre right. At the top of the picture is part of the drop zone. Courtesy of the Imperial War Museum.

Epilogue

George Parry's death was not reported back in the UK until June 28, when his name appears in the List of Casualties in *The Times* and other newspapers. Leonard Moseley's article appeared in a number of newspapers around the country over the next couple of days. The extract used in this booklet is the original version from the Daily Sketch for June 29, 1944 under the headline *"Padre Fell Beside Men He Tried To Save"*.

A version of his article was also printed in the Chelmsford Chronicle the following day. It was prefaced with comments from the Bishop of Chelmsford:

> *This is a great shock to me. It is like a personal bereavement....*
>
> *I had known him from his boyhood. He had irresistible personal charm. Everyone who knew him called him 'George'. He was one of those you instinctively call by his Christian name. It seems such a tragic thing to lose young men like that. He was sincerity and goodness blended.*

As the Bishop of Chelmsford says, everyone who knew him called him George. In fact, he did not like being called Mr. Parry. In the obituary Reverend John Stanley wrote in the St. John's Parish Magazine for August 1944, he says:

> *...I still treasure a letter from him which begins: 'My Dear Vicar, - For heaven's sake give up calling me 'Mr. Parry!' I am not used*

> to it – so from now on please let it be George. I was baptised with this name, not by Parry!'

This article is the reason for calling him George wherever possible and appropriate throughout this booklet.

On July 1, George's Obituary, written by the Bishop of Barking, appeared in *The Times*.

Ten days later, on July 11, Sir Herbert Williams, the Conservative MP for Croydon South asked a question in the House of Commons over the circumstances of the death of Reverend George Parry. Sir James Grigg, Secretary of State for War said that the circumstances were being investigated. The results of the investigation are unknown.

On Sunday July 9, the normal service of Mattins at St. John's was replaced by a memorial service for George. It was attended by a great many people and the address was given by the Bishop of Barking, the Right Reverend James Inskip. The August 1944 parish magazine records that they came to the service to:

> ...show their love and respect for one who had ministered so faithfully in this parish and elsewhere.

The collection for the service was given to the Airborne Forces Benevolent Fund and it raised more than five times what would normally be expected at an 11am Sunday service.

In the obituary Reverend John Stanley wrote for the Parish Magazine he has this to say about George:

> All his gifts he used to the glory of God in his work amongst us, and no more fitting tribute has been paid to him than that which came from a group of boys, tracking him as a possible spy in the Invasion scare days of 1940. 'Let him pass, he's all right, he's a real parson, he is.'

George is buried in Benouville Churchyard, Normandy, grave no. 21.

After the war was over, George was posthumously awarded the standard medals for his service. These were:

> 1939/45 Star
> France and Germany Star
> Defence Medal
> War Medal

The medals were issued on March 25, 1950 and sent to his mother. His father had passed away in 1948.

George's brother, Major Allen James Maule Parry, was also with the Airborne troops on D-Day. He was in charge of "A" Company of the 9th Parachute Battalion, who were tasked with destroying the Merville battery. George's brothers Allen and Roden both survived the war.

Memorials

George Parry's name appears on the following memorials:

The Royal Army Chaplains Department Memorial, Museum of Army Chaplaincy, Amport, Hampshire

The Old Weymouthians War Memorial, St Aldhelm's church, Weymouth, Dorset

The King's College London War Memorial

The Roll of Honour for 1939 - 1945 in St John the Baptist church, Leytonstone, London

The Roll of Honour for 1939 - 1945 in Emmanuel church, Forest Gate, London

The green altar frontal for the High Altar of St John's, Leytonstone was given by George's mother in his memory. It was dedicated by the Bishop of Barking at the Sunday morning service on June 16, 1946, Trinity Sunday.

Picture 14: The RAChD Memorial at Amport. George is remembered in the bottom centre section. Courtesy of the Museum of Army Chaplaincy.

Sources

I am grateful for the information and assistance provided by the following sources:

The Museum of Army Chaplaincy
Airborne Assault Museum, Duxford
Imperial War Museum, London
The National Archives, London
London Borough of Bexley Archives
London Borough of Bromley Archives
London Borough of Waltham Forest Archives
Essex Record Office
Dorset History Centre
St Aldhelm's Church, Weymouth
Wellingborough School
Hansard
Army Personnel Centre, Glasgow

The Pegasus Archive – www.pegasusarchive.org
ParaData – www.paradata.org.uk
The Kings Collection – www.kingscollections.org
Commonwealth War Grave Commission – www.cwgc.org
The British Newspaper Archive – www.britishnewspaperarchive.co.uk
The Times Archive - www.thetimes.co.uk/tto/archive
Ancestry – www.ancestry.co.uk
Find My Past – www.findmypast.co.uk
The Genealogist – www.thegenealogist.co.uk

St John the Baptist, Leytonstone parish magazines for 1938, 1939, 1940, 1941, 1943, 1944 and 1946
St John the Baptist, Leytonstone Registers of Services covering 1938 to 1946
The Quarterly Army List: October 1941
The Clavinian, 1929 to 1933

The Pegasus and Orne Bridges: Their Capture, Defences, and Relief on D-Day by Neil Barber, 2009, Pen & Sword Books Ltd.
Here's to Our Far-Flung Empire: An Account of Colonial Upbringing by Tony Orchard, 2010, Memoirs Publishing
The Tale of Two Bridges adapted by Barbara Maddox, from the diary of Colonel R.G. Pine-Coffin, 2003, Published by Peter Pine-Coffin
One Single Poppy by Daphne H Carr, 1997, Falcon Books

Picture 15: Jenni Crane with George Parry's Suitcase.

Acknowledgements

In researching this booklet, I have received help from a number of people in various archives, museums and libraries and I would like to thank them all for their assistance.

This booklet would not have happened if it were not for certain individuals. Reverend David Britton asked me about putting an article on the church website and this was the seed that spawned the research. Alasdair Preston did so much to locate references to the events of the airborne assault on D-Day and Army Chaplains, particularly on the web. Stephanie Deudney, who wrote the original article about George for St John's December 2009 parish magazine. And of Course, Jenni Crane, the BBC researcher who bought George's suitcase in March 2014 and started her campaign to find out more about him, without which none of this would probably have happened. I am grateful to all of them.

John Wilson

THE DAILY SKETCH, THURSDAY, JUNE 29, 1944

FRENZIED NAZIS BAYONET OUR WOUNDED PARATROOPS

Padre Fell Beside Men He Tried To Save

From LEONARD MOSLEY
With the Allied Forces

THIS is the story of one of the most brutal actions perpetrated by the Nazis against our troops fighting in Normandy—the story of how German soldiers broke into a medical aid post filled with our wounded in the Orne Valley on D-Day, killed the helpless men and then murdered the Padre who tried to defend them.

The padre who gave his life in an attempt to save his wounded charges was the Rev. George Edward Maule Parry, of the 6th Airborne Division.

Captain Parry, formerly of St. John's, Leytonstone, and Emmanuel Church, Forest Gate, was 29 years of age and was killed by a knife or bayonet. His parents, Canon A. J. and Mrs. M. C. Parry, live at Wanstead. His brother, Lieut. Peter Francis Maule Parry, was killed in North Africa in November, 1941.

Here are the details of the Nazi murder raid on our wounded men, so far as they could be pieced together for me in Normandy by officers and men of the 6th Airborne Division, to which I was attached at the time as a war correspondent.

Cut Off From Help In Bitter Fighting

The Parachute Division was given the job in the early hours of D-Day of dropping by parachute and capturing intact the vital bridges spanning the river Orne and the Caen Canal. Padre Parry dropped with them. Soon all were engaged in defending themselves against some of the bitterest and most determined Nazi counter-attacks of the invasion.

Hearing that "A" Company of the battalion holding the perimeter of our defences along the west side of the canal near the village Le Port was in sore straits and aid for the wounded was badly needed, Padre Parry set off through the darkness to join them.

Not long after he arrived Nazi forces infiltrated between the company and the rest of the battalion, cutting them off from all help.

Soon after dawn a panther tank and self-propelled gun opened fire on them, taking heavy toll of the men.

"A" Company's commander was so badly wounded that he carried on the direction of the battle from a stretcher.

All efforts to get help from the rest of the battalion failed and many men died in trying to get through.

Placed Himself Between Wounded

And then after one attack the enemy broke "A" Company's line at one point and p e n e t r a t e d sufficiently to reach the medical aid post, where Padre Parry was working on the wounded.

Those who were near enough to see what happened say that the Nazi troops, who seemed to be in a completely frenzied condition, set upon the wounded, shooting a n d bayoneting them.

Padre Parry immediately went to the aid of the helpless Britons lying on the dressing station floor.

He protested vehemently against the murder of the helpless paratroopers and when this was ignored by the enraged Germans he is believed to have tried physical intervention and put himself between the Nazis and the wounded troops.

He was then charged by the enemy troops and in the struggle that followed bayonets or knives were used by the Nazis and Padre Parry was cut down. He fell beside the men he tried to save.

Owing to the desperate situation that prevailed at the time it was impossible for anyone else in "A" Company to go to his aid or to the aid of their comrades and for several hours afterwards the medical post was in No Man's Land.

Not till later in the morning did the second in command of the company manage to reach battalion headquarters and tell his story.

The Rev. George Parry

Despite his wounded shoulder he crawled through the gardens and shell-wrecked houses of Le Port and dodged through the Nazi lines until he reached the bridge.

There he refused to have his wound dressed, but asked for a patrol and immediately returned to his company fighting the whole way back. It was this patrol which recaptured the medical post and occupied it. They found all its occupants dead, with Padre Parry lying beside them.

Then with this small reinforcement "A" Company held off all subsequent Nazi attacks until late in the evening of D-Day when troops from the beaches fought their way through and relieved them.

Not A Man Who Did Not Want Revenge

Padre Parry was immensely popular with his men, and news of his death and the way in which he died sent a wave of fury and indignation through the whole division.

The paratroopers had been fighting magnificently, but they fought even more finely after that.

I was with the men of the battalion during many hours of D-Day watching their successful battle to hold the bridge and I know how deeply they felt the loss of the man who had dropped with them in the dangerous darkness of the night before.

I don't think there was a man in the whole battalion who that day did not fight to avenge the death of Padre Parry.